HELEN MARIE BYRNE

ALL ABOUT THE HORSE

18th September 1974

novum pro

© 2024 novum publishing

ISBN 978-3-99146-848-6
Editing: Charlotte Middleton
Cover illustration: David Mulroy
Cover design, layout & typesetting:
novum publishing
Internal illustrations, author's photo:
David Mulroy

The images provided by the author
have been printed in the highest
possible quality.

www.novum-publishing.co.uk

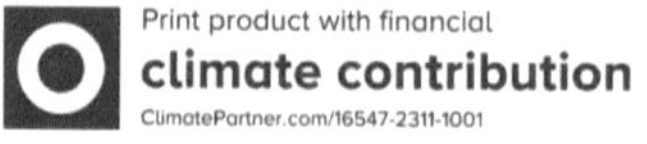

Contents

What is a Pony? 7
Shoes 10
Shoeing 11
Some of the Horse's Ailments 12
Fitting Ponies' Saddlery 15
Cleaning Tack 17
Feeding Your Pony 18
Grooming Kit 20
How to Tell the Age of a Horse 23
Conformation of the Face 24
Colours and Marking of the Horse 27
Twelve front views of a horse's head 28
Bits 30
Bridle 31
Breeds 32
Reader's Crossword Puzzle 38
Pony Island 39

My Book is All About The Horse

September 18th 1974

What is a Pony?

Scientists call all the breeds and types of horses and ponies by their scientific name, Equus (ek-wus), which means 'a horse'. From the earliest historic times, however, ordinary people have named the different horses which they recognised. They named them according to their ages, sizes, types, and by the places where they lived, such as Shetland, Dartmoor, Arabia, and so on. Young horses which were very small were given nicknames such as 'tyke', which is used in the north of England, but more widely they were called 'pony'. The word probably comes from the French word 'poulenet', which means 'foal' or 'young horse'. Gradually, grown horses began to differ in size, and the name 'pony' stuck to the little horse. The more ancient and wilder breeds, especially ones like the British Mountain and Moorland breeds, were called ponies. In America, they have cow ponies. Because the game of polo was first played on very small horses, they were called polo ponies. The name is still used, although the horses now used are much larger.

Nowadays, a horse is said to be a pony if it is over a certain height. From the fifteenth century, horses' heights were shown as so many handfuls or handsbreadths. This is the depth of the palm of the hand. The measure of one hand is now fixed at four inches (4.8 centimetres). A pony now must not be more than fourteen hands two inches (one hundred and forty-eight centimetres) high.

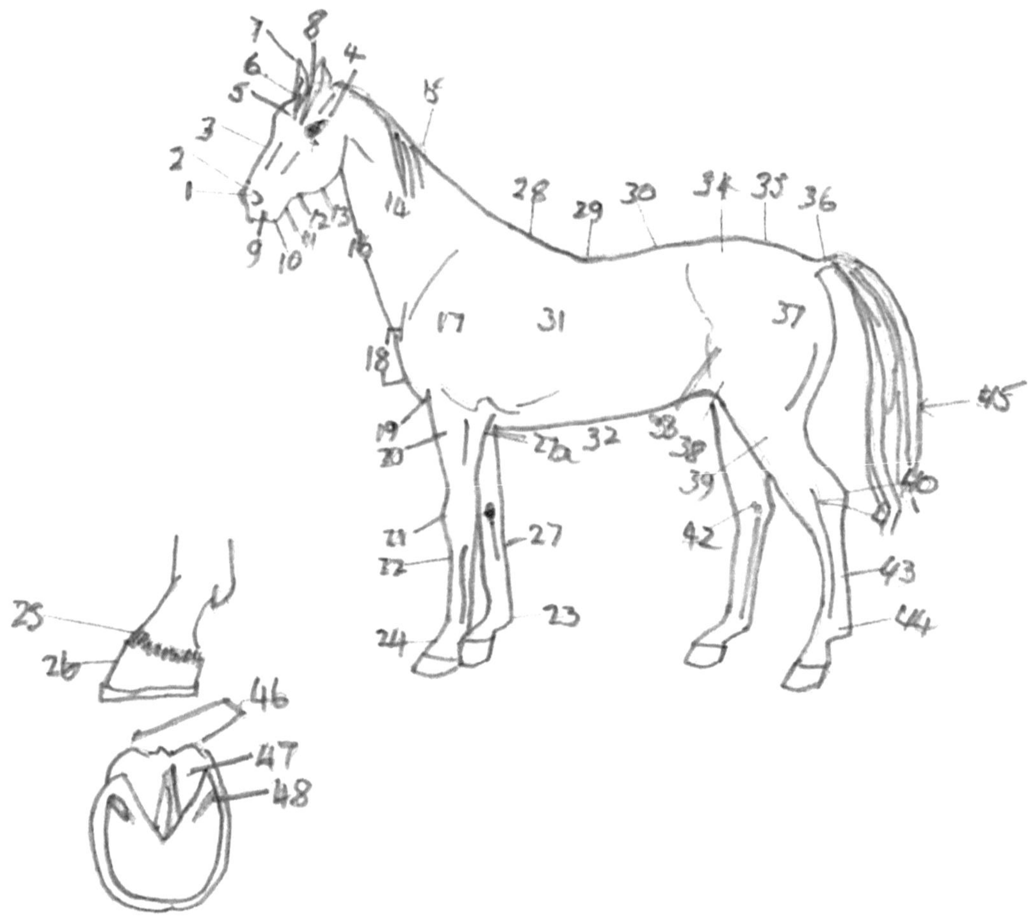

1. Nostril	19. Breast	36. Dock
2. Nose	20. Forearm	37. Hip joint
3. Face	21. Knee	38. Stifle
4. Eye	22. Cannon	39. Gaskin
5. Forehead	23. Fetlock joint	40. Point of hock
6. Forelock	24. Pastern	41. Hock
7. Ears	25. Coronet	42. Chestnut
8. Poll	26. Hoof	43. Cannon
9. Mouth	27. Tendon	44. Fetlock
10. Chin	27a. Elbow	45. Tail
11. Chin groove	28. Withers	46. Heels
12. Jowl	29. Back	47. Frog
13. Cheek	30. Loins	48. Burs
14. Neck	31. Barrel or ribs	
15. Crest	32. Belly	
16. Windpipe	33. Flank	
17. Shoulder	34. Point of hip	
18. Point of shoulder	35. Croup	

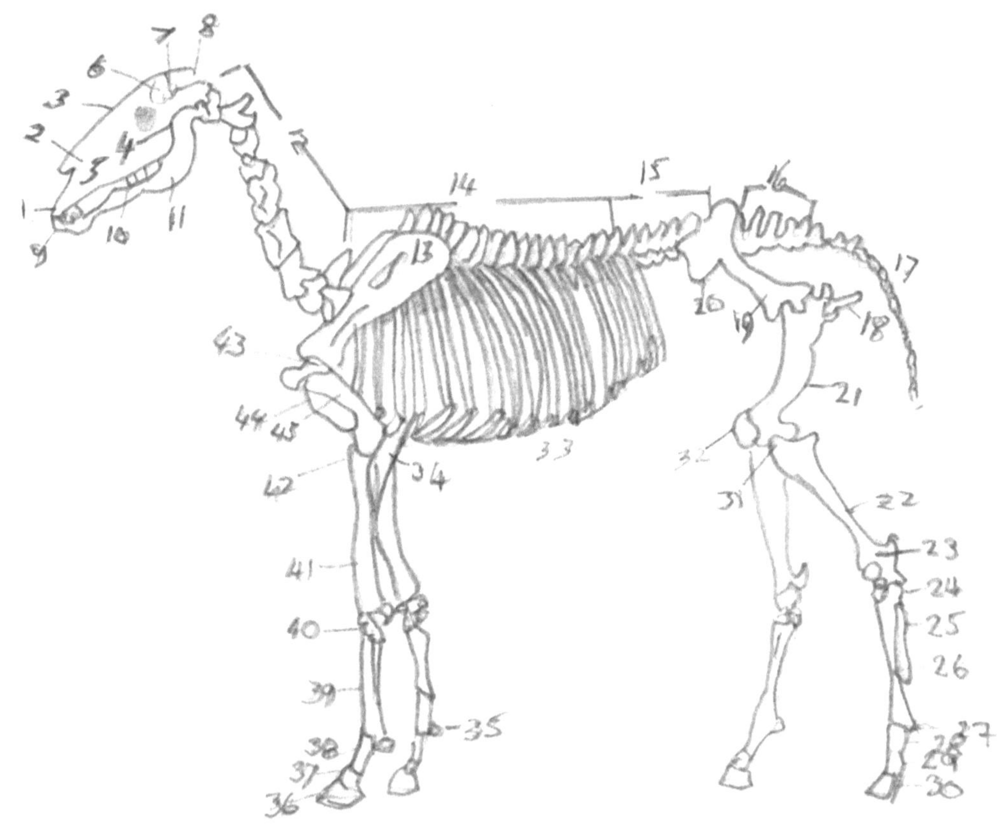

1. Premaxilla
2. Nasal bone
3. Maxilla
4. Zygomatic bone
5. Frontal bone
6. Parietal bone
7. Coronoid process of mandible
8. Occipital bone
9. Incisor teeth
10. Molar teeth
11. Mandible
12. Seven cervical vertebrae
13. Scapula
14. Thoracic vertebrae
15. Six lumbar vertebrae
16. Sacral vertebrae
17. 18–12 caudal vertebrae
18. Ischium
19. Ilium
20. Trochanter
21. Femur
22. Tibia
23. Os calcis
24. Astralagus
25. Splint bone
26. Cannon bone
27. Sesamoid bone
28. Large pastern
29. Small pastern
30. Pedal bone
31. Stifle
32. Patella
33. Ribs
34. Radius
35. Sesamoid
36. Pedal bone
37. Small pastern
38. Large pastern
39. Cannon bone
40. Knee joint
41. Radius
42. Ulna
43. Humerus
44. Sternum
45. Shoulder joint

Shoes

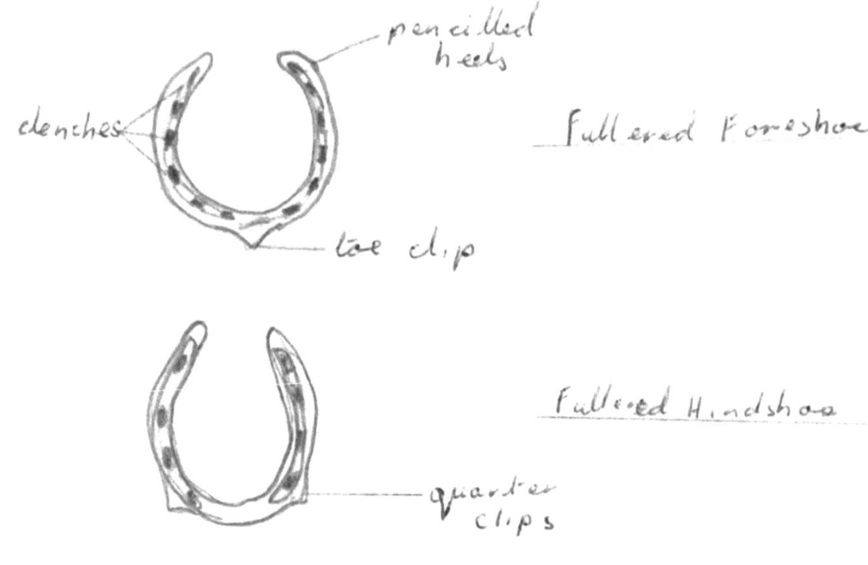

Note the hind hoof should always be allowed to protrude a little over the edge of the shoe.

Hind shoe with calkin

Clench

Shoeing

The Right Type of Shoe is Important

A fullered shoe, which has a little groove indented round it, is best for all riding purposes, as it is light and non-slip. The fore shoe should have pencilled ends to prevent the hind shoe from catching and pulling it off, and it should have a toe clip in the centre. The hind shoe should have quarter clips on either side instead of in the centre so that the hind foot may protrude a little over the end of the shoe to prevent the horse from striking and injuring its own foreleg. Both shoes usually have more clenches (nails) on the outside than on the inside.

A fullered hind shoe with calkins (high heels) is sometimes advisable. The heel supports the back tendons and is especially helpful in the case of heavily built cobby ponies. Calkins also give extra braking power when jumping and act as an additional aid to prevent slipping.

A flat machine-made shoe should never be used. It is heavy and slippery and only suitable for carthorses doing slow work.

Some of the Horse's Ailments

The horse has many ailments, and I have listed some of them.

Laminitis

Ponies get laminitis by being left out in a large meadow and then eating too much grass.

Symptoms

1. The first symptom is that the pony will lie down very frequently. It is natural and very beneficial for ponies to lie down every day, but they seldom stay down for more than half an hour or so, and they usually choose the early morning for their resting time, so if you see your pony lying down more frequently and for longer periods than this, watch it carefully, for there may be something wrong.
2. The second symptom is that the pony's feet will feel very hot to touch, especially the forefeet. Have shoes removed and then lead the pony over some hard, stony ground. If it walks tenderly – just like a cat on hot bricks – then you may be quite sure it has laminitis coming on.
3. The third symptom – should you fail to notice these earlier signs of laminitis developing – is that the pony's poor feet will gradually become so painful that it will hardly be able to hobble at all, and it will squat down on its haunches – just as a dog sits down – with its forefeet stretched right out in front. When things have reached this stage unnoticed and unattended, the pony will probably have a high, feverish temperature as well.

The Cure

Bring the pony into a comfortable stable at once, with a good, deep bed. Have its shoes removed – if you have not already done so – and *starve* it. Give it plenty of clear water to drink – a bran mash with Epsom salts, if it will take it, may help. After this, just two days, when the pony is feeling a little better, as it should be after forty-eight hours of this treatment, increase the hay, according to size, up to four or five very small feeds a day. Keep the pony on this diet until it walks absolutely soundly again and no longer flinches when led over hard ground. Then, when you do put the pony out into a field again, begin very gradually, allowing it only half an hour's grazing the first day, gradually working up to the ration it should have had before it became ill.

But forever after one attack of laminitis, a pony's diet will have to be very carefully regulated, for it will, in the future, be very susceptible to the same trouble again. In addition to this internal treatment, some people advocate standing the pony in a stream for an hour or two daily, or on a bed of cool clay. But though these remedies may help to lessen the pain in its aching feet, they do not constitute a cure, which must be dealt with from within. Nothing can really prevent the tragic after-effects of a severe case of laminitis, when the sole of the foot will drop and bulge – turning convex instead of concave, as is the sole of a healthy foot – making the pony unable to shoe.

This is why laminitis should be avoided at all costs, and why the search for a smaller field is wiser than risking the pitfalls of wide acres and rich pasture.

Worms

There are two main symptoms of worms to look for.

Symptoms

1. Your pony's tummy may look fat but its ribs will show, especially as it moves, and there will be little hollows beneath the hip bones (the pony will be tucked up).
2. The pony may be listless in behaviour, have a deep, dry cough, or continually rub its tail.

The Cure

Pick up some of the pony's fresh droppings, seal them in a tin and send them to your vet. The vet will have them analysed and will send you the appropriate dose with instructions as to how to give it. Never attempt to concoct a dose yourself – it may do more damage than the worms! And remember that ponies who have access to hedgerow plants are less likely to harbour worms. They themselves will seek out male fern and wild garlic, which are nature's safest antidote.

Splints

These are small, hard lumps of bone which usually form on the forelegs and cannon bones and make the pony lame. They are very common in young ponies which have been ridden too far and too fast for their age or broken in too young by too heavy a rider.

Give the pony complete rest for many weeks. Massage with iodine oil or ointment or any veterinary product made specially for this purpose.

Curb

This is a lump, which starts small, no larger than a pea. If neglected, it soon becomes as big as an egg. It forms just below the hock joint on the hindleg and makes the pony lame. Both cause and cure are exactly the same as for splints.

Windgalls

These are little puffy swellings – again starting as small as peas but soon growing as large as an egg – round the fetlock joint. The cause is usually too much uncollected (slapdash and unrhythmical) trotting on hard, high roads, especially when the pony is coming home tired. Again, the cure is the same as for splints and curb.

Fistulous wither

Pay attention to saddle fitting.

Fitting Ponies' Saddlery

If a pony's saddle does not fit properly, not only will the pony feel so uncomfortable that it will be obliged to buck and probably develop other bad and unseating habits in legitimate protest, but it will also very soon hone in the shoulder, or if it is a larger pony with a prominent wither, it may even be afflicted with a fistulous wither, an unpleasant malady, hard, sometimes impossible, to cure. It starts in the guise of an ordinary saddle gall just over the wither and develops, if unheeded and neglected, into a dangerous abscess, which forms beneath the skin and is inclined to penetrate deeply between the shoulder blades. In olden days a very painful and not always successful operation was considered to be the only cure. Now it can often be tackled much more safely and humanely by injections. All these troubles come quickly and are prolonged, meaning the pony will be out of action for many weeks, often months. So it behoves all pony owners to make sure that their saddles fit.

Points to remember

1. When the rider is mounted, the front arch, or pommel, must neither press down upon nor pinch the pony's back or wither.
2. The back arch, or cantle, must not press down unduly upon the pony's loins.
3. The saddle flaps must not impede the progress of the shoulders.
4. No part of the saddle must press upon the spine. You should be able to see daylight right down the channel when the rider is mounted.
5. The saddle must not be far too large for the pony just to accommodate much too heavy a rider.
6. Take good care that your pony never rolls with its saddle on. If it does, it will break the tree for a certainty, and a saddle with a broken tree bears down heavily on the pony's spine, soon causing injury. It is hard to tell if a tree is broken or not. If in doubt, take the saddle to a saddler to be examined.

Girths

Girths must also be given careful attention or they too will rub and gall. They must not be fastened so tightly that they cut into the pony's skin, nor so loosely that the saddle sways about. If a girth is hard and misshapen through lack of cleaning, it will very soon rub and cause trouble. And it must be borne in mind that ponies who have not been ridden for some time and whose skin has become soft must be very carefully and gradually introduced to the saddle again, just as, if you, having worn nothing but your bedroom slippers for two or three months, suddenly donned a pair of hobnail boots and went for a ten-mile tramp, what blisters you would have the next day!

Bridles

Bridles must fit properly too!

1. If the browband is too tight, it will make the pony continually shake its head as it rubs and irritates its ears.
2. If the bit is too small, it will pinch the pony's poor lips and hurt its mouth to such an extent that the pony may try to bolt or rear. Just like bucking with an uncomfortable saddle, which has its origins in genuine pain or discomfort, bolting and rearing are habits which, once formed, are hard indeed to break.
3. Too large a bit will slide from one side of the pony's mouth to the other and be equally uncomfortable. As the type of bit used will depend entirely upon the capability of the rider and stage of training or schooling reached by the pony, advice or suggestions on this do not come within the subject matter of this little book.

Cleaning Tack

Cleaning tack, as cleaning saddlery is called, must be done regularly, or every time it is used, for badly kept tack soon cracks and breaks and lets down the rider in more ways than one!

When very dirty and caked in mud or sweat, bridles must be taken to pieces completely, each piece laid out on a table and well scrubbed with a small brush and tepid water. Hang the bridle in a warm place to dry (not on top of the hot kitchen stove). When dry, rub in saddle soap with a damp sponge. Polish off the bridle with a stable rubber or piece of soft, clean rag or chamois leather.

Every day and always after, used tack should be rubbed over with saddle soap, which will keep it soft and pliable. Exactly the same treatment applies to the saddle, only do not over-polish the seat of the saddle. Saddles are hard enough to stick to as it is, without having them highly polished! Web girths must be well brushed with a hard brush, string girths washed periodically, leather girths cleaned as any other tack, and a piece of flannel sprinkled with neat's-foot oil folded inside to keep them extra soft.

Feeding Your Pony

If you are looking after your own pony, work out a routine for yourself and stick to it. Don't feed your pony when you feel like it or worse still forget to feed it more often than not. There are some golden rules about feeding, and there are many technical books about stable management, but these are the basic principles.

- Water before you feed.

- Feed little and often, if possible.

- The Chief Feeding Stuffs

Oats

Best fed crushed or rolled, as they are easier to digest.

Bran

Good broad bran is best, containing plenty of flour. Dampen slightly to feed, or give as bran mash. Bran is useful to help digestion in a tired horse; it acts as a laxative. Boiled linseed and one tablespoonful of Epsom salts may be added and given once a week.

Horse nuts

Horse nuts are an excellent balanced ration for horses and are not so heating as oats, but they are very expensive.

Chaff

Chopped hay added to the feed adds bulk.

A feeding table approximately per day for a pony of 14.2 hands, ridden by a child of thirteen.

New Zealand Rugs

When correctly used, New Zealand rugs can be a very useful adjunct to the combined system (layering of rugs), for by using one, a pony, living under the combined system, which would normally be obliged to keep its own winter coat for protection when running out during the day, can be clipped or half-clipped. If a pony is needed for hunting or for fairly fast work, it should wear a New Zealand rug to keep it warm when it is turned out. This rug is windproof and waterproof and is made so that it cannot come off if the pony rolls, as would of course happen if one attempted to turn a pony out in its ordinary stable day rug. Just like a stable rug, the New Zealand rug should be properly fitted, by a saddler if possible, as individual adjustments are often needed. If the rug does not fit, it will soon rub and gall, as well as becoming dangerously displaced when the pony walks.

New Zealand rugs, if incorrectly used or abused, can be very harmful. They must not be put on and left on by a careless pony owner who verily imagines they are as good as a mobile stable! They must be removed for a reasonable period each day to allow air to get to the pony's skin, and the pony must be thoroughly groomed and the inside of the rug well brushed and cleaned, and all the straps kept saddle-soaped and oiled to keep them soft. Otherwise, the unfortunate pony will soon suffer all manner of sores and be covered in lice – very unpleasant!

There is, however, one very grave danger in the use of a New Zealand rug. Unless the pony has been very carefully introduced to the rug and is absolutely accustomed to wearing one before it is turned out, in windy weather the wind will get under the rug, making it flap and billow, making strange noises, which will absolutely terrify the pony. Many are the serious accidents which have happened this way. The pony will make a mad charge to try to rid itself of this demon upon its back. It will try to jump any barrier which happens to loom in sight, because of the rug. The pony will find too late that it cannot raise its forelegs and so down it will come with a crash, probably resulting in serious injury.

So before a pony is trusted outside in a New Zealand rug – much less turned loose in a field in one – let it get absolutely used to wearing the rug first in the stable, then lead the pony out in it in all weathers, in calm and storm, then try it in a small field or enclosed yard and watch the pony's reactions when it is alone and the wind gets under the rug, and finally, when the pony no longer shows the slightest sign of alarm, then and then only, venture to turn the pony out in it.

Grooming Kit

Grooming

A complete grooming kit consists of several items.

1. Dandy brush
2. Body brush
3. Water brush
4. Curry comb and rubber curry comb
5. Wisp
6. Sponge
7. Stable rubber
8. Mane combs and tail comb
9. Hoof pick
10. Hoof oil

Reasons for grooming

Firstly, you can really alter the appearance of a pony if it is properly turned out, clean, with trimmed heels, and pulled mane and tail. Secondly, it is better for the pony, because it keeps it in healthier condition and free from disease.

Technique

When grooming, start at the neck, then do one side and then the other, leaving the pony's head until last of all. First use the dandy brush for removing mud and sweat, then the body brush with curry comb, sponge the eyes, nose, dock, and finally use the rubber for the final polish.

Tack cleaning kit

1. Soap
2. Bucket
3. Duster
4. Metal polish
5. Chamois leather
6. Soap sponge and water sponge

Grooming kit I

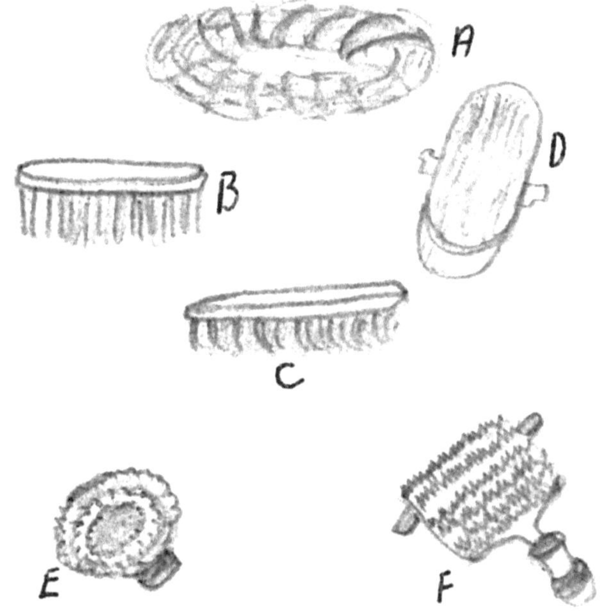

A Wisp
B Dandy brush
C Water brush
D Body brush
E Rubber curry comb
F Curry comb

Tack cleaning kit

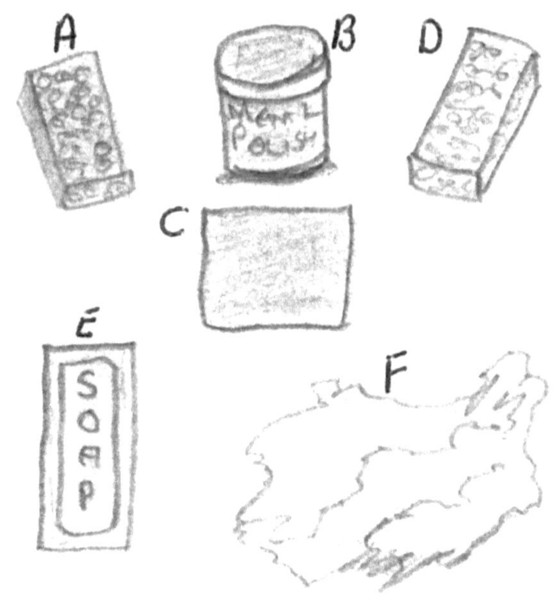

A Water sponge
B Metal polish
C Duster for polishing
D Soap sponge
E Saddle soap
F Chamois leather

Grooming Kit II

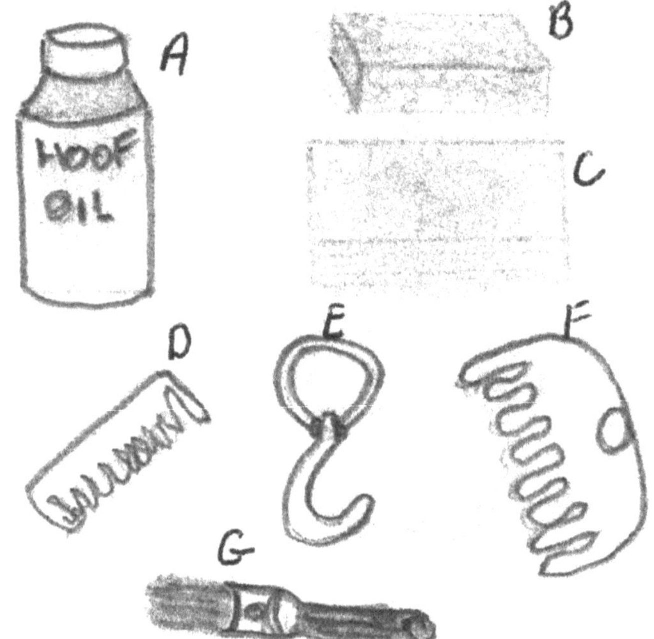

A Hoof oil
B Sponge
C Rubber
D Mane comb
E Hoof pick
F Tail comb
G Panet brush

How to Tell the Age of a Horse

The age of a horse or pony can be told by looking at its teeth. Like humans, horses grow milk teeth then permanent ones. At two years, a horse has a full mouth of first teeth, then at three years old it sheds some of them and they are replaced by permanent ones. Other teeth fall out at four and five years, and in this way experts can tell the animal's age quite accurately up to the age of eight years. When a horse reaches nine years, it is called 'aged', because from then on one cannot tell the age so precisely. A horse has been known to live until the age of sixty-two!

The age of a horse is indicated by the shape and markings of its teeth.

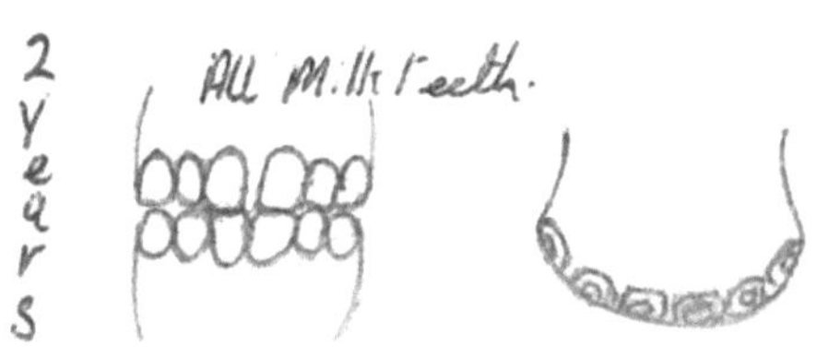

Two years / All milk teeth

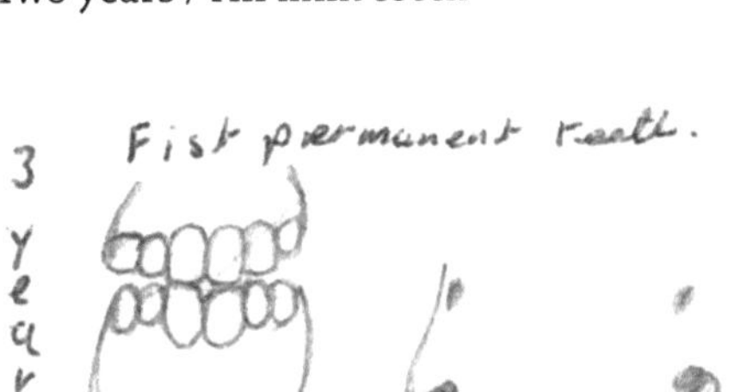

Three years / First permanent teeth

Four years / Last milk teeth

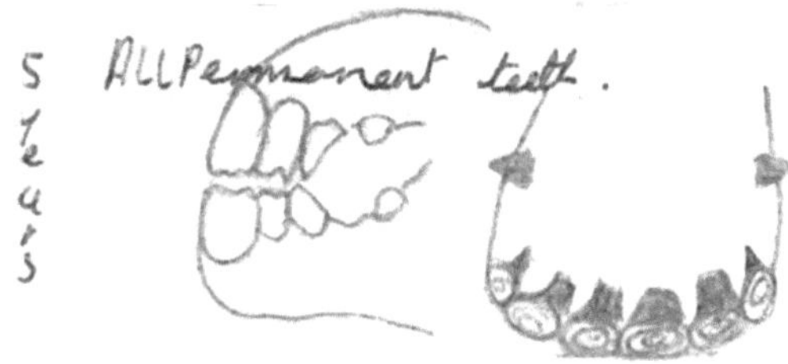

Five years / All permanent teeth

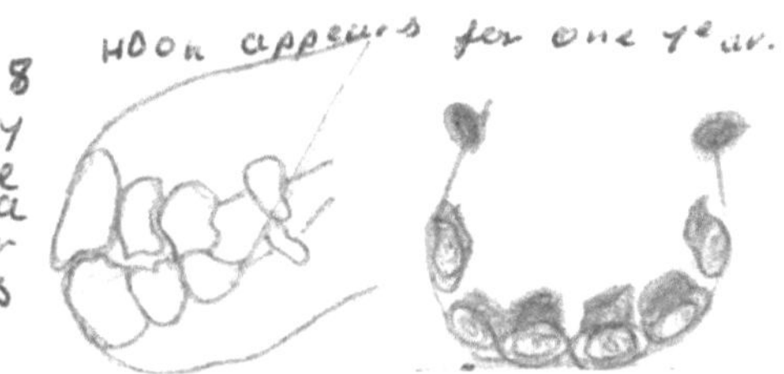

Eight years / Hook appears for one year

Ten years / Black groove appears

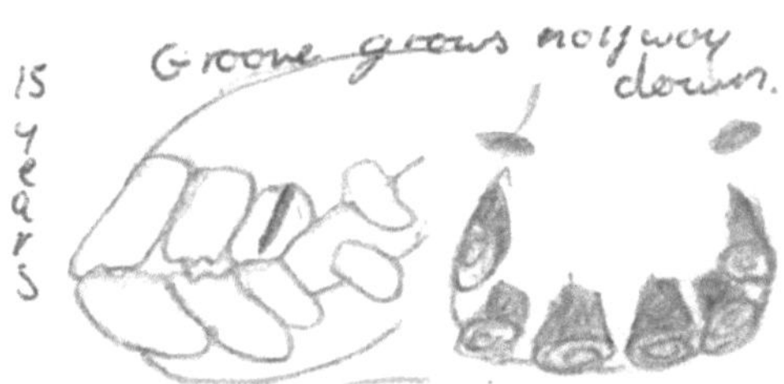

Fifteen years / Groove grows halfway down

Thirty years / Groove disappears

Conformation of the Face

Concave face

Roman nose (convex face)

Straight face line

Correct position

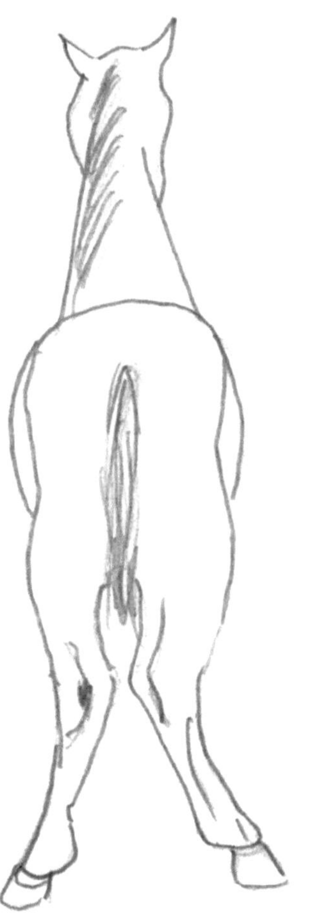

Cow-hocked

Sickle-hocked

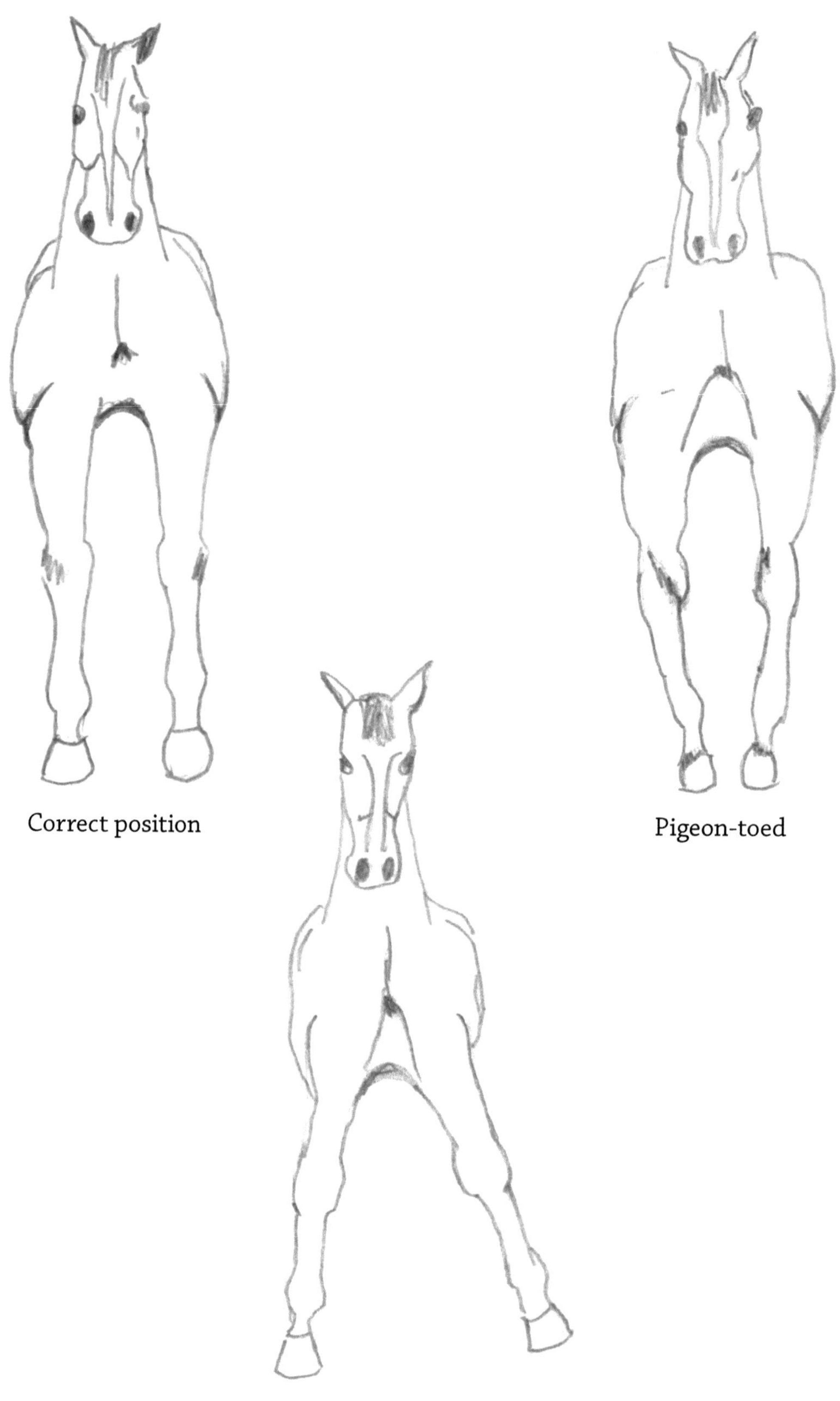

Correct position

Pigeon-toed

Wide in front

Colours and Marking of the Horse

Toad eye and muzzle

Mealy eye and muzzle

Twelve front views of a horse's head

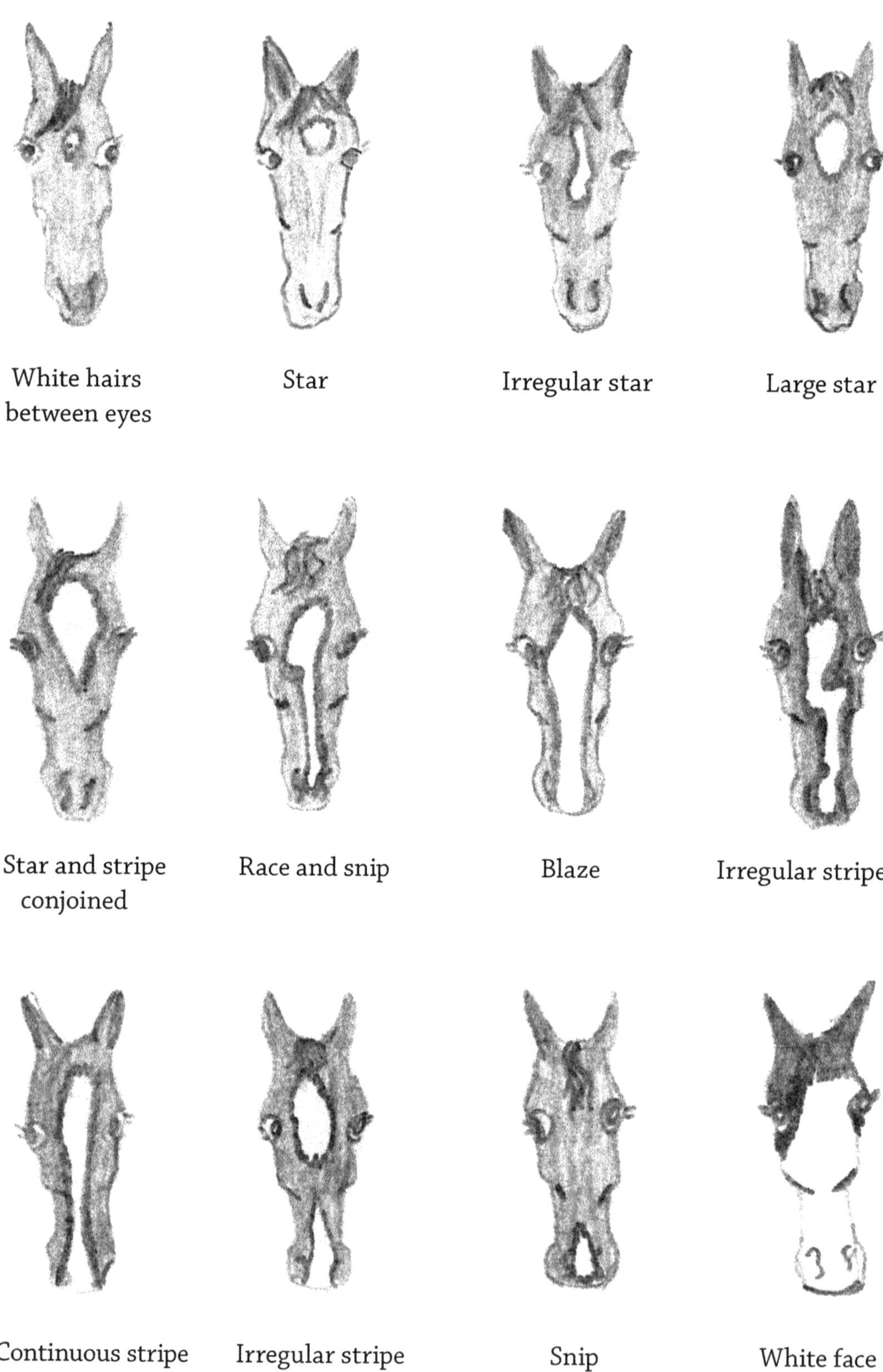

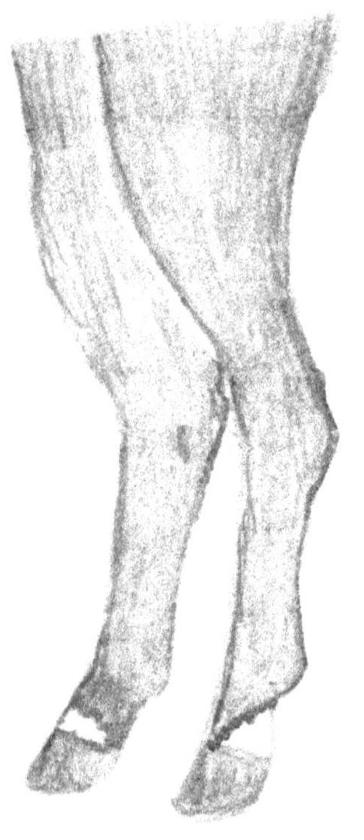

Coronet heel

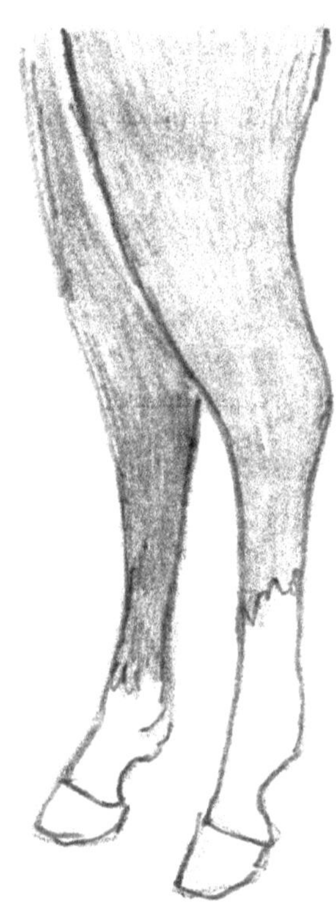

Sock stocking

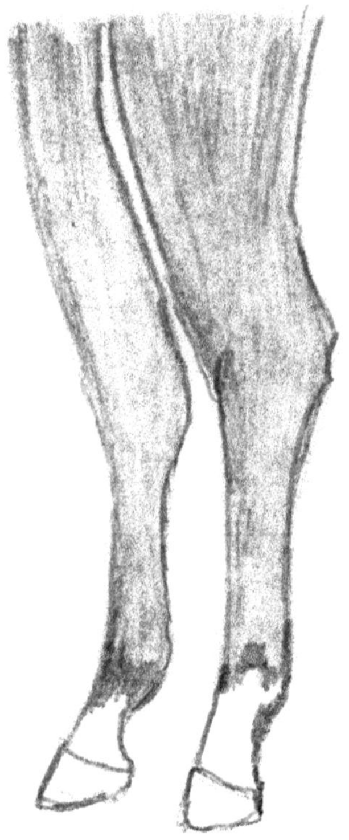

Off-hind partly pastern

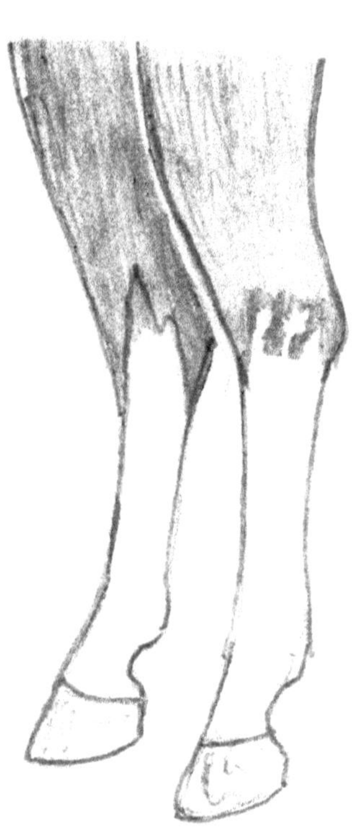

Legs

Bits

A bit is a metal bar worn in the horse's mouth. Each end of the bar is attached to the bridle and the reins. Since a horse's mouth is very sensitive, the horse will feel every little movement or pressure on the bit when the rider moves the reins. Using the reins, their legs and body balance, the rider 'talks' to the horse and tells it to turn right or left, to go faster or more slowly, to stop or to start, and other instructions. There are many kinds of bit to suit different horses and different purposes. The simplest of all is called a snaffle.

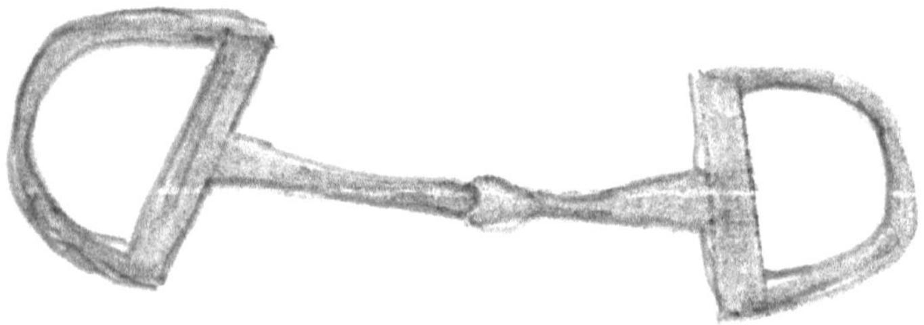

A jointed snaffle

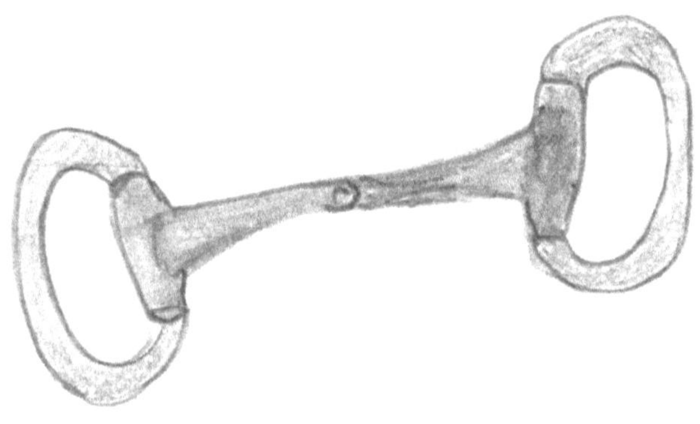

An Eggbut snaffle

Bridle

A bridle is the leather headpiece worn by a horse when it is ridden or driven. The reins and bit are fitted onto the bridle, although there are some bridles designed to be used without a bit. The double bridle can be used with several types of bit. Blinkers are sometimes used to prevent the horse seeing too much to the side and on horses which work in harness in traffic.

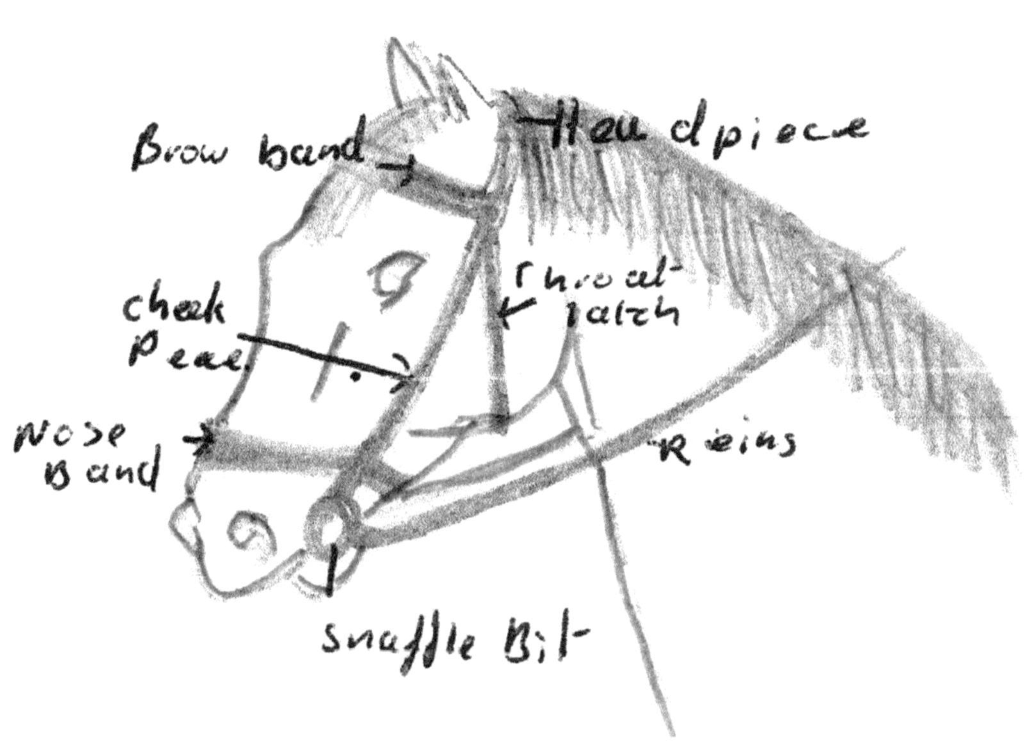

Breeds

Anglo-Arab

This is the result of a mating of pure Arabian and Thoroughbred. This is a recognised breed in Great Britain and in France, where it was first developed. M'Lord Connolly, European Horse Trials champion, 1962, and Ali Baba, Olympic show-jumping gold medallist, 1952, are notable species of this breed.

Appaloosa (Ap-pal-oos-a)

The Appaloosa is a spotted horse, whose markings were first recorded in the prehistoric era. It takes its name, however, from the North American district Appaloosa in the states of Idaho and Washington, where it was specially bred by the Nez Perce Indians. Spotted horses are popular in Great Britain and the United States. There are societies devoted to breeding them.

Arab

The Arab is a unique breed, which has become, through its descendant, the English Thoroughbred, the foundation of the modern riding horse all over the world. It is called Arab because it has been bred in the Najd plateau of Central Arabia for two centuries. It did not start in Arabia but came from the north, in the areas now known as Iran (Persia) and Russian Turkestan. The Arab peoples have been very careful about keeping the type pure. No horse was accepted in a pedigree unless it was Kehilan, or purebred. From this has come the name of its western descendant, the Thoroughbred.

The pure Arab is marked with some unique points. The front of its head curves inward so it is 'dish-faced', and it has a short, wide head and large eyes. It has one fewer bone (five instead of six) in the backbone between the last of the ribs and the croup. This gives its short well-ribbed-up appearance. It has two fewer bones in the tail (sixteen instead of eighteen). This causes that well-known gay, high carriage of the tail. Its height is usually 13.2 hands to 14.2 hands (137cm–147cm). It was the fastest horse in the world until overtaken by its own child, the Thoroughbred. The speed of the Thoroughbred is combined with the great power of endurance, and it still wins long-distance races. The Arab was introduced into England as a breed in the middle of the nineteenth century by the poet Wilfrid Scawen Blunt and his wife, Lady Anne Blunt. They founded the famous Crabbet Stud in Sussex, which is still active. Arabs are now bred all over the world as well as in Arabia.

Clydesdale

This heavy horse breed takes its name from the old name for the area of Lanarkshire round the River Clyde. It was first bred in the middle of the eighteenth century from local horses and imported Flemish heavy horse stallions. It is distinguished by the amount of white on its face and legs. The chief colour is bay (brown and black).

Cob

The cob is not a breed but a type of horse or pony whose special mark is a solid square-looking body on short legs. Cobs used always to be docked until the Docking and Nicking of Horses Act 1949 made it illegal in Great Britain. Docking is cutting the tail very short so it is only five to eight inches of dock.

Connemara

The Connemara is the ancient breed of Ireland, found now in Connaught, west of Lough Corrib and Lough Mask, and north of Galway Bay. It is one of the mountain and moorland breeds of the British Isles. The original prehistoric blood has become mixed with Arab, Spanish, and other blood. It is still used for carrying peat and sea-weed in packs but is also an excellent riding pony. The height is thirteen to fourteen hands (132cm–142cm), and the colours are mostly grey, black, bay brown, and dun.

Dales

A Dales pony is a strong breed of pony, originally a pack carrier, bred mainly in the upper dales of Tyne, Wear, and Tees, below Hillhope Hill. They are a powerful cobby build, up to 14.2 hands (147cm), with strong, short, well-feathered legs. The main colours are black, brown, and bay. They are much used today for riding and especially pony trekking, because of their ability in hilly country.

Dartmoor

The Dartmoor is a pony breed probably dating from the Bronze Age. It used to run wild on Dartmoor, the highland between the north and south coasts of Devon. Nowadays the ponies on the moor are of a mongrel type mixed with Shetlands. The modern-day Dartmoor ponies are mostly bred away from the moor. Their height is not over 12.2 hands (126cm). They are sturdily built with nice small heads and are easy action. They are used as riding ponies and as foundation stock for cross-breeds.

Exmoor

The Exmoor breed, which for thousands of years has occupied the high plateau of Somerset, has never been mixed with any other breed. It is probably the purest descendant in the British Isles of the ancient prehistoric types. It has the mealy mouth of the wild horses of the pictures in the coves of southern France. Dun is the most common colour, but they are also bay and brown. Its maximum height is 12.3 hands (129cm).

Falabella (fal-ab-ell-a)

The Falabella is a breed of miniature horse bred during the last hundred years by the Falabella family on the Recreo de Roca ranch, outside Buenos Aires in the Argentine. No records have been kept, but it was probably the result of breeding again and again from the smallest animals, until now it has a maximum full-grown height of thirty inches (75cm). This makes it the smallest-known breed in the world.

Fell

The Fell pony is a little like a Dales in appearance, although the Fell is the shorter of the two. It is native to Westmorland and Cumberland. These tough ponies have a history of hard work in carrying lead from the mines. They are friendly animals and very popular as children's mounts. Fell ponies usually grow to about 13.2 hands (137cm) and are black, dark bay, dark brown, and occasionally grey. The hair on the mane and tail is long and curly.

Manipur

The Manipur breed is descended from the ponies of Mongolia, with possibly some Arab blood. It is found in the district of Manipur in Assam, India. It is a pretty pony and very strong for its size – eleven to thirteen hands (111cm–132cm). It was on these ponies that modern polo was first played by Englishmen in the middle of the nineteenth century.

Mongolian

The Mongolian is the original foundation breed of nearly all the horses of Asia, spread over the states of Inner and Outer Mongolia. This area is bordered by Manchuria on the east, Turkestan to the west, Siberia on the north, and Tibet and China to the south. It is a wonderful animal, very strong for its size, very fast running and with tremendous powers of endurance. Its height used to be about 13.3 hands (139cm), but in recent years it has been mixed with Arab and Thoroughbred and has grown bigger. Mongolian ponies are exported to China for racing and other sports, and the numbers are increasing.

Mule

A mule is the offspring of a male donkey and a female horse. Strong and hardy, it is still used in several parts of the world for carrying goods, and occasionally people, over rough country. A mule is sometimes stubborn – that is why a stubborn person is sometimes called 'mulish' – but can live on rough food and needs little attention.

New Forest

The New Forest ponies inhabit the area of forest and heath in the southern part of Hampshire. Once, this forest extended much more widely over the south of England, and the ponies were probably like the Exmoor and the Dartmoor. Many different breeds have been added so that the present breed is a mixture. Now no other breed is allowed in the forest, where the ponies run free and seem wild. Like all the mountain and moorland breeds they are strong and hardy. Their height ranges from 12.2 to 14.2 hands (137cm–147cm).

Oldenburg

The Oldenberg is the largest of the German warm-blood breeds, standing 16.2 to 17.2 hands (168cm–178cm). Bred in Oldenberg and East Friesland, it is of mixed blood, but one line of its pedigree goes back to Eclipse, an undefeated eighteenth-century British Thoroughbred.

Palomino

Any horse or pony which has a gold colour with a dark skin and silver or flaxen mane and tail is called a Palomino. It is now connected with America, but the colour can be found in horses all over the world. In Spain, horses of this colour are known as Ysabellas, named after the queen of Spain, who financed Christopher Columbus' voyage to the New World. The American name is said to come from Juan de Palomino, who was given one by the Spanish invader, Hernando Cortes. To be perfect, the colour must be that of a newly minted gold sovereign.

Percheron

A Percheron is a breed of heavy-form horse first bred in Le Perche, France. It is now popular all over the world, particularly in England. It is always grey in colour, has short legs without any 'feather', and is very powerful and docile.

Przewalski's Horse (Jher-al-ski)

The wild horse of Asia was first found in the Kobodo district of Mongolia, north of the Altai Mountains. It was discovered in 1881 by the Russian explorer, Colonel Przewalski. Live specimens were first brought to Europe in 1902. The height is about twelve hands (121cm). It is of a dun or reddish-brown colour with a mealy (oatmeal) muzzle, a dark stripe from the mane along the backbone, black points and a tufted tail. Its short upstanding mane with no forelock is one of its outstanding features. It has rather donkey-like feet and a heavy head. It is probably the sole survivor of the prehistoric horses of Asia.

Quarter Horse

The Quarter Horse is a North American breed, so called because it was able to sprint very fast in the quarter-of-a-mile races organised by the early American colonists. Its ancestor was an English Thoroughbred James, imported into Virginia in 1956. When the West was opened up, the Quarter Horse was used as a cow pony, especially for cattle cutting (singling out animals from a herd), and later for polo and general pleasure riding. Its height ranges from fourteen to fifteen hands (142cm–157cm). It has now been exported to Australia for cattle drafting.

Shetland

The Shetland is the smallest breed in the British Isles. Its natural home is in the Shetland Islands, but it probably belongs to the same group as the ponies of Norway, Iceland, and the Faroe and Lofoten Islands. It is extinct in the last two places. Scant living in hard conditions probably stunted its growth. It is very strong for its size, and its top height is forty-two inches (103cm – note that it is not measured in hands).

Shire

The Shire is the biggest of the four great breeds of heavy horses in Great Britain. It is probably descended from a mixture of English horse and the heavy horses from Flanders, developing to its present size from the eighteenth century onwards. The principal breeding areas have always been the counties of Lincolnshire, Cambridgeshire, and Huntingdonshire. The main colours are bay and brown, with a lot of white on the legs. The height is over seventeen hands (173cm). It weighs over a ton and can pull a load of five tons.

Thoroughbred

The Thoroughbred is the leading breed of the world. It was bred in England in the eighteenth century from horses brought from the East. The three main fathers of this breed were Arabian horses known as the Godolphin, the Byerley, and the Darley, from the names of their principal owners. The famous racehorse, Eclipse, was descended from the Darley Arabian. The Thoroughbred is found in every country in the world which has horse racing. The names of the horses are kept in special books called stud books. The first stud book was the English one, and it is called the General Stud Book. Practically all modern breeds of horses have Thoroughbred blood.

Timor

The Timor is a very small breed of pony which inhabits the East Indian island of Timor, just north of the state of Western Australia.

Welsh

The Welsh is the native pony of the principality of Wales. Records of this breed have been kept for one thousand years. The original stock has been mixed with Arab or Eastern blood. There are now three types. The smallest is the Welsh Mountain, which is not more than twelve hands (121cm) high. West is the Welsh pony, and the height limit is 13.2 hands (137cm). The third type is the Welsh cob. This can be any height. All the ponies have a showy, high action when trotting.

Zebra

The zebra is a special member of the horse family found in Africa. The mane is said to come from the Amharic (Ethiopian) word meaning 'striped'. The mountain zebra comes from South Africa. Grey's zebra comes from Abyssinia and Somaliland. Burchell's and Chapman's zebras come from South Africa. It is a relation of the Quagga, which is now extinct. These types have full stripes but in different patterns. The Quagga only had stripes in front.

Reader's Crossword Puzzle

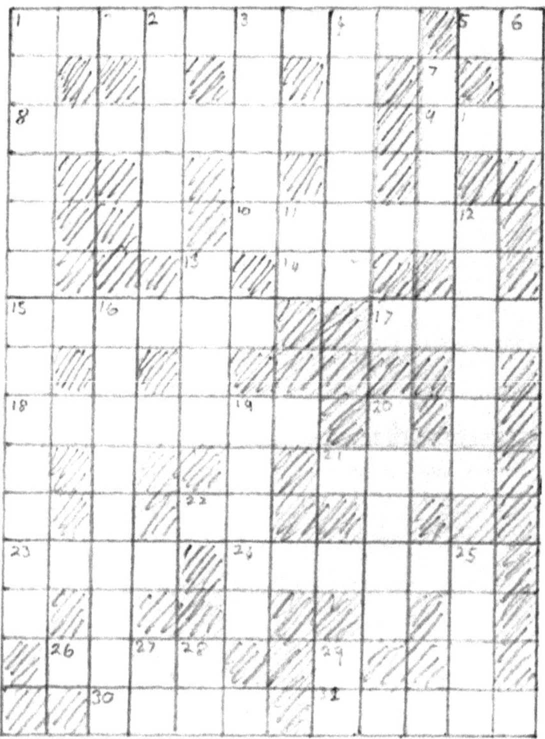

Across

1 The tendon of the gastrocnemius muscle (9)
5 Pronoun for the horse but not the mare (2)
8 Shin disease (8)
9 Teeth are useful to determine this (age)
10 Equine accommodation (6)
14 Common word of exclamation (2)
15 For causing pain (6)
17 Type of fodder (4)
18 Fault in conformation (3,4)
21 Most people like to ... horses (4)
22 Abbreviation for 'human vet' (2)
23 Funny yet not humorous (4)
24 Used to keep a rug in place (6)
26 Spurs and crops are ... (4)
30 Ponies sweat to keep them like this (4)
31 There are several variations of colour in this horse (5)

Down

1 Ancient horse (15)
2 Tit-bit (5)
3 Carrots are these (5)
4 Often made of sheepskin (6)
6 A good horse has a kind one (3)
7 Fly swat (4)
11 ... and fro (2)
12 Stallions (6)
13 Measurement of fields (4)
27 ... or don't (2)
28 Me far ... la te (2)
29 One ... the other (2)

Pony Island

There is an island far away,
Of which you have not heard,
It's tranquil through the night and day,
You hear not man nor bird.

The wind blows over hill and vale,
The tides leave beaches bare,
A quiet clip-clop can be heard,
Of a pony and his mare.

These are the last of one great herd,
Their pride and joy, a foal.
Their one last chance of keeping up
A breed of long ago.

One more foal was born one spring
As the mare died one warm day,
These two grew up and had one more
As the father went away.

He was never to return,
His foals were left to starve,
The breed that thrived on the fair isle
With homes no more than caves.

These three ponies turned to four,
And five, then six, then more,
The herd is growing strong again,
They're seen to trot the shore.

The author

Helen Marie Byrne was born in Morewnstow in Cornwall and worked as a groom for Mendip Farmers' Hunt until the age of twenty-one, when she retired due to illness. Helen loved horse riding and scuba diving. She possessed an in-depth knowledge of horses and wrote the book All About the Horse at just sixteen years old. She is missed by all who knew her.

novum PUBLISHER FOR NEW AUTHORS

The publisher

> *He who stops
> getting better
> stops being good.*

This is the motto of novum publishing, and our focus
is on finding new manuscripts, publishing them and
offering long-term support to the authors.
Our publishing house was founded in 1997, and since
then it has become THE expert for new authors and
has won numerous awards.

**Our editorial team will peruse each manuscript
within a few weeks free of charge and without
obligation.**

You will find more information about
novum publishing and our books on the internet:

w w w . n o v u m - p u b l i s h i n g . c o . u k